H O M E W O R K

HOMEWORK

JOE ELLIOT

 Lunar Chandelier

ISBN: 978-0-9846076-2-4

Lunar Chandelier Press
323 Atlantic Avenue, Brooklyn NY 11201
lunarchandelier@gmail.com

Design & typesetting by HR Hegnauer | hrhegnauer.com
Interior text typeset in Bembo.
Colophon designed by David Borchart.
Author photo: Jennifer Witcher, 2010.

Some of these poems have appeared previously in:
Hanging Loose, Ocho, The Poetry Project Newsletter, and *Boog Lit Reader #2*

Lunar Chandelier Press
Brooklyn, NY

Delirious Avenues
lit
with the chandelier souls
of infusoria
– Mina Loy

For Leo, George, and Walter

Anonymous

Nostalgia

For although
our telescopes

magnify a great
many times,

even the nearest
planet is so

far away that
the largest

in the world
would not

show us
living creatures,

supposing that
they are there.

Fantasy

You don't
want to

make it.
You want

to be left
behind.

Your hut,
your patch

of beans.
Either way,

you do
or you don't

want to,
or neither,

earth
underneath.

The Room

A bed
a set of drawers

a throw rug
two paintings

a chair
a table

and on the table
a lamp.

That's it.
Cordoned off

the crowd
inflamed

may look
to its heart's

discontent until
every drop

of inborn order
has drained

from their eyes,
and unable to

blink, move,
or even rot,

they're sold off
as accents for

yard and garden,
merchandized

as lantern-holding
jockeys for

the front door.

Cosmic Narcissism

When you
look up

and pull on
my Saint

Gregory the Great
medallion with

your little fist
I can see

a canopy
of leaves

shiver,
the actual

sun splintering
through

in your eyes.

Ornithology

I hear a splash
and turn my head.

The bird is already
leaving the water.

The man is already
turning the corner.

That part of the dream
already out of reach.

Already the paper,
folded and sheathed,

landing on the porch.
He must not want me

to see his killing.
I must not have been

prepared to see it,
to receive it unspun.

And Yeah

A little night music
spills from the absent

middle-schooler's backpack
in the hall. A call

must be coming in.
A pleasant enough ring,

the usual requirement
of getting to know by

getting it, note by note,
wrong, lifted. The sky

clears. Spring must be
a coming in. Hello? Yes,

meet me at eight. I'll take
all the mountains, all the trees,

all the rivers and streams
and whatever attendant deities

you got, and yeah, throw in
a dozen roses.

Remember,

the action figure
does not act

or move in relation
to the boy

who holds it;
they are one.

No, it leaps and kicks
only in relation

to the world
surrounding the boy.

For he lets fly
his full-throated

Hiyah! as it lands
its deadly karate

chop to the carotid
of the household

love they live in.

Homeland Security

The purple and green
patch of cabbages

by the old portcullis
is ready to pick.

The individual violets
bordering a path that runs

around a corner and along
the outer fortifications to

the public bathroom,
by the entrance to which

they crowd and widen
into a welcoming bed,

are lovely. Sweet geraniums
at the fort's center

encircle a weathered
toddler-sized shell

whose tip points up,
while a double bed

of pink and blue pansies
on either side guard

a steep set of stairs
down to what was once

a magazine but is now
an office. And there,

just outside the door,
ready to be deployed,

a tray of rust-colored
begonias rests on top

of a few stacked bags
of compost and mulch,

and the new caretaker,
tilting his chair back

against a six foot thick
wall, is reading a book.

Their Stories Do Not Concern Us Here

For a brief moment,
at the beginning

and end of each day,
heaven spills

out into the world.
On either side,

high curving walls
of tentative delay,

of trees and weeds
that waving manifest

the wind's unendingness,
that shut out the grid,

the suddenly unthinkable
grid that extends,

just a few feet
on the other side

away, for miles, and all
the millions of lives

therein, from the eye
of this sinuous,

high speed, bumper
to bumper serpent.

When I visit
her garden and see

the flowers that bloom
like clockwork,

one after another,
to the right height,

for the right duration,
complimentary colors

separately amassed,
I am impressed,

and think of the white
foam and floating leaves

and sticks rubbing
up against the dock,

and how the world
vibrates, and how that thing

in her voice makes me
do what she wants,

and how none of us
knows anything,

really, and wonder
if it wasn't motor oil

and not water that poured
out of Jesus'

wound in his side
on the cross.

Two

A crow flies by
out in the open

through some trees,
behind a roof,

a few seconds
of nothing, and then

out in the open,
is a whole play.

Of course, your applause, your
putting on your coat

and getting up to go
but then bending over

behind some seats
and then standing back up

with a hat
on your head,

is also a play,
as surely as the aisle

and the crowded lobby
and then the door

to the outside is also a few
seconds of nothing.

The electric light
by the door at the top

of the stairs is still on.
The white plastic deck chairs

arranged in a semicircle
on the terrace are waiting.

On the low sea wall,
half hidden by the leaves

of an old buttonwood
stubbornly anchored

into the coral below,
a solid jade replica

of some Egyptian bust,
half man half woman,

looks on. Behind her
the sea is rising.

Behind him dawn doesn't
break but seeps

into day through huge
vertical thunderclouds

and misty sheets of rain
moving this way

across the water.

In The Basement

Seemingly out of the
top of the head of

a middle-aged man
of average height

and average build
and average features

sitting at a desk
telling us his story

with an openness
that is so palpable

we are opened too,
and up the poorly

plastered and thickly
painted wall behind him,

a cockroach crawls
slowly and steadily

making its way toward
a gaudily framed

portrait of Jesus,
circa 1965,

long-haired, handsome, pale,
unbelievably kind,

taking its time
as if its tiny insect

soul relished this bit
of effrontery, this perfect

scene thievery, until
hesitating at the edge

of the golden frame
with its feelers, disappears.

It's

It's not just the bodega
that has transformed itself

into an internet café.
The whole neighborhood's changed.

Everyone you see on the street
seems to walk with a livelier step,

seems put together
a little better,

with smarter clothes
and a greater stake

in himself, and that stake goes
straight through his heart.

The man behind the counter,
nicely groomed and also undead,

hands me my double latte.
It's everything I could ask for:

frothy and cheerful,
leaving just the slightest

virtually metallic
taste in my mouth.

Last night thunder
shook the house

for over an hour
before the drumming

rains finally came.
The Earth Mother

is not a figure
of speech.

We are not worthy
of speech,

but sometimes she suffers
us to sleep

deeply in flimsy
ccts in the cellar.

We Were Waiting For

For Mel Glenn

Chaucer, of course, opens in the rain
Cummings is always mud puddle wonderful in the rain
Bergman and Bogart are standing in the rain
The Germans in their trenches and the French in theirs
are separated by a mere field of mud in the rain
Covered in newspapers a man is asleep on a bench in the rain
Heaven is reaching down to marry Earth in the rain
and Henry is training Eliza to articulate in the rain
In fact, each time it rains rhymes with every other time it rains
Huddled together, Adam and Eve are leaving in an early morning rain
Moses is parting the Red Sea in a light, but steady rain
Anywhere in Paris in the late afternoon in the rain
Zig-zagging beads are tracing patterns down the windows of cars in the rain
The sky being pierced and pierced in a puddle in the rain
Williams pulls over on the road to the contagion hospital to write a poem in
     the rain
Making your mind up in the rain
Taking your hat and then your coat off in the rain
How the craziest ideas, even the Ark, begin to look a little better in the
     accumulating rain
In the shameful, all-forgiving rain
Caught red-handed in the rain
Letting it all fall apart in the rain
Turning your back and walking away in the rain
Gene Kelly is always halfway up a lamppost in the rain
Mothers everywhere are standing in doorways calling their kids to come in
     out of the rain
The inside when outside all is enshrouded in billowing sheets of rain
The steady, drumming rain
While upon his crumbling kingdom begins to fall the first few drops of a fat
     new rain
By definition, the brainstorm begins to brew in the incipient rain
Jesus is walking, just like a human, home in the rain
Fumbling for your keys in the rain

Snowmen melt in the rain
Giving in to the rain
Everything is equal in the rain
Walking together but not holding hands in the rain
The non-judgmental rain
Gibson and Weaver are watching Jakarta fall in a blinding rain
At the edge of the continent Alexander has begun to weep in the
    obliviating rain
Thus, Irish footballers are ever upended in the rain
Everywhere people are falling asleep to the lovely sound of rain
Trying to light a match in the rain
Sticking your tongue out in the delightful rain
Looking out a basement window on an plaza in Bucharest in the rain
In what is now Pottersville, Jimmy Stewart stands dismayed in the rain
Near Kilimanjaro, Hemingway stalks a version of himself in the self-hating rain
Across the street a car is parked in the all-day rain
As Christmas decorations persist in the rain
Delayed on the tarmac in the rain
While so much comes down to a tin can in the rain
Romulus and Remus being suckled by an enormous wolf in the rain
Going out to make a call on the corner payphone in the rain

The Russian Titov

The language of mythology
is always unambiguous.

This is how
the invisible works.

This is a stream.
This is a cliff.

The good is divided
from the bad in

just this way, of course.
But there was something

which I now fancied
I dimly perceived

and grew frightened.
There is a tree.

There are its leaves
and fat apples,

and his seventeen orbits
around the earth.

This is the earth.
This is your body.

Both are round
and slightly plump,

and plumply invisible.
I grew invisibly

habitable too, and dreamy
and lay down on this

mythological earth,
your unambiguous body.

Actual Outline of a Vague Shape in the Backyard

Oscillating fan. Not a metaphor,
not a chiropractic adjustment of
your psyche. Water pump hums
a tune called habit but this time
you happen to hear it. It's liquidy
and almost unbelievable. Downstairs,
cats padding around jump off of
something. Thump. In another room,
low voices stop, and then furniture
being pushed a limited distance,
and then start up again. The amount of
effort and energy required to paint
and prop up scenery, hang lights
and pump in music, when there already
is a world. You don't know it, but
becoming, for a moment, aware that
you don't, you become curious,
desirous to venture out into it,
tentatively. There it is. It is there
without you, but wants you. There
is something that wants you but
doesn't depend on you. The refrigerator
in the dark kitchen is an inundation.
The steam heat pushing up through old
pipes is a beaming influx of light.

Advice Machine

For JB

Don't be attached to the future.
Don't worry about things

on your list of things
to do. Don't think about

getting up to do something.
Don't think about departing.

Stop loving death. Stop
embracing your own dissolution.

Stop fucking rot. Stop sticking
your cock into the corpse of

your illusions. Stop pumping
madly into the orifice

of your fears. Stop trying to
get off. Get on. Get on up.

We Always Love

and the things
that we love
tell us what
we are,

and the things
that we hate
are also things
that we love,

but, in this case,
to hate, and so
also tell us
what we are.

The Hype on the Back of the Book

comparing it to the Iliad. O idiot commodity
among commodities, O ready-made memory
among memories cut bound boxed and stacked
on a skid in a warehouse somewhere
in the Meadowlands have mercy on us!
O puffed up interests and cookie-cutter
enthusiasms of the half-eaten and barely awake
come to our aid! May not a little but all
of your maggotty hyperbole bless us!
May a whopping assembly-line dollop of
your shrunk-wrapped desire interchangeably
fuck us and make us, for a moment, feel
whole! Yes, may your soon to be remaindered
and shredded leaves multiply without end,
blindly and to no purpose! May the resulting
burgeoning cloud of confetti choke the air
and fall on the heads of the crowd, ten deep
on either side of the parade, at the heart
of which an empty box already waiting
for you, you not yet shelved, not yet even
conceived of, on the back of a flatbed
slowly processes by and is cheered wildly,
"The King is dead! Long live the King!" Yes,
may the glue in your spine rise in our throats!
May the latest interactive graphic dazzle us
into collective coma! May our heart rates slow
to the point where we at last understand
deeply the phrase "Buy me and be loved!"
May your vortex of narcissism and desire,
boundary and rage, be not wasted, but be
re-worked into protracted and glorious war
in the Middle East! Yes, may the killing
of these others, these inventions of our
appetite, be the price of your love! Please!

We need you! May you bankrupt all of us
to satisfy what is now every six by nine
laminated individual's right to fifteen seconds
of fame! Hurry! May your twin signatures
of paint-by-number envy and fear be stitched
into a publicity blitz, into a cataclysm of
page six anagnorisis! Yes! May you fill us
with shallow awe! May you fool us
completely so that we no longer even see
that it's actually we who are winking at
our own machinations on our own behalf!
O shameless panderer, we love you! Please,
kiss our ass through this darkest night of
willful ignorance so that we may increase
in the pretense of being saved, so that we may
applaud this pulpy pantomime of the outside!
O wishful thinking and crow-barr'd,
all-in-caps agreement to scratch your back
if you scratch mine, O magical fingers
of the marketplace—and we know how very
partisan you can be—may you lovingly
crinkle our cellophane souls! May your
revolving door of bestseller after bestseller,
of exclamation mark after exclamation mark,
longingly press the top ten buttons
on the production boards for each of our
personalized full-scale Broadway numbers!
Yes, it's time to stand up and deliver!
May your demographically determined
karaoke life defy gravity! May it float over
our cardboard cut-out heads and entertain us
for the next few moments leaving us galvanized
and nailed to the authorial/denial wheel
in the fluorescent basement of a crumbling
affirmation factory also somewhere
in the Meadowlands! And when, at last,
should we wake up one day a little sickened

and bloated, should we look up at the prompting
cards and recognizing them as such be too tired
to pretend to believe, should our faculty of
wanting and getting, of justifying and pretending
and wanting and getting, ever wear out,
then may the wrath of Achilles be rewoken,
then may he drag behind his chariot outside
the walls of Troy our consumerist corpse
through the dust! Then may the last vestige
of humility, this scintilla of self born of that dust,
retreat into its tent and refuse parlay.

February 24

Aside from a few compulsive types
out in the middle of the night

shoveling the sidewalk and brushing off
their SUVs so that it's just

that much easier to do the job
again in the morning, the streets

are empty. The snow is falling
through the conical and regularly spaced

streetlight in a kind of slow motion
pantomime of nothingness. So much

relentless activity descending without
weight or sound, a silence that grows,

accumulating without effort or impact,
covering everything. The limbs of trees,

newly obliterated, have become more
noticeable, gestural, figures caught

in mid-supplication. The demarcations
of sidewalk street curb are gone,

and the cars have begun to mound,
become unknown or even owned,

while front stoops and garden hedges
are already weird volumes thrusting

up to greet this lowering silence.
But look! How sad! Halfway down

the block you can just make out,
through the storm's muffled scrim,

Old Glory! Not that it's unpatriotic
to leave her out flying all night

and during weather, for these days
we're told to be ever-vigilant, and so

it's not unfitting that she sometimes go
without sleep or experience a little

hardship; no, it's that all this peace,
all this white is interrupted by

the red of those stripes, and it's sad
they cannot let go of this identity

for even a few hours, but must insist
on themselves, on these empty stars

in a field of deep, corporate blue.
And it makes me a little angry, too;

but maybe, if I tell you about it, here,
as I walk, I can get some of that sweet

stillness back, and maybe those guys
are just like me, maybe they're just

guys: their day is over, their kids
are asleep, and they just want to get

out of the house, out of the well-lit
and definite cave, and see something

else before going back inside
and getting into bed, and, instead

of taking a walk or lying down
on their backs and making angels

in the snow, they gave themselves
the excuse of a little work, "Honey,

I'll be back in a few. I've gotta go
out and clear the walk. We don't

want anybody slipping and breaking
their necks." And maybe they just love

peace, overwhelming white,
the idea of everything they know

being blanketed and erased,
bedded down and silenced.

That Country

The poet travels with the circus
and gets to read his home-cooked epic
between the human cannonball and the lions,
although nobody can actually hear him
because of the Jumbotron's tremendous din,
the barkers crying their bags of crackerjacks,
and kids crying for more while their parents
talk about what they talk about: who
did what to whom and how to avoid that
mistake; and also because he has to compete
with those clowns in the third ring doing their
fire brigade routine which turns out to be funny,
but in a way that elicits and then exploits fear;
but mostly because nobody gave him a mic.

And yet, if he does okay, if this image
of someone standing about 100 yards away,
ignored and inaudible, but nevertheless
continuing to speak to what he considers
his audience, this assembly of 25,000
unwitting citizens, moves somebody else
enough to get up out of her seat and stretch
her legs or pay a visit to the snack bar
or restroom, then they give him a shovel
and bucket and he gets to clean up after
the elephants, which, I suppose, to be
in the service of—forget about that fat
guy with the cigar—such sad and intelligent
creatures, creatures with such thick skin
and huge ears, must be deemed an honor.

Either it's cold and bitter,
heat escaping from a thin,

insufficient atmosphere into an ever
expanding vacuum, in which, were it not

for the impossible suit you have to
put on and maintain at all times,

checking nozzles, levels, adjusting knobs,
adding a little bulk to whatever spot

looks like it might one day develop
a leak, you would even more quickly

expire. Or it's sheer beauty.
Empty brilliant winter blue sky,

bright brutal proud presiding sun,
tangible moist billowing warm breath,

icicled beard, shivering fierce
sweet surprising wind peeling back

the pretense that it's okay, acceptable
low-level misery boredom, do-able

self-effort worry failure fear. No,
either annihilation or joy. Choose.

A hat is what you'd need
to keep me on your mind.

A badge on your chest is what you'd require
to gain admission to that much denial.

A boat is what your heart desires,
your hollow body waving from the beach.

A fresh coat of paint will always speed
the process of crossing that one off
your list of things to forget.

Dancing back to back with truth is a pleasure
for which the smoothest footwork and
a scripted sense of humor are prerequisites.

Watching himself on a monolithic screen
as he struts into the end zone is an act
that demands half a stadium of pixelated others
cheering wildly, but no one else.

The sacrifice of that much fantasy to make your life
a little more real and empty is an act
that demands half a stadium of pixelated others
cheering wildly, but no one else.

A coffin is what you'd be opting for
when you say, "I want to be left alone."

A capitol is what you'd be wearing
as a helmet on your ever-expanding
head when declaring war on terror.

Not an SUV or a 401K or the GNP,
but a child is what you'd need
to grow and send overseas.

A four-car garage is now the minimum
shelter needed to secure that much rancid ideology.

For that kind of motion is the kind of motion
that desires more motion.

For a bigger something in every something
is the knee jerk prayer of the faithful.

For the blade of the faithful, honed on the stone
of fear, must be placed on the throats of
the faithful for the faithful to declare their faith.

For a fateful event is the sine qua non
when tucking the sleepy populace into a bed
of automatically watered perennials.

For that old boot could be that something
left in the backyard to fill with rainwater,
if only you'd finally allow it to happen.

For abject surrender to the finite is what
seeks you not seeking it.

For if I walked in the door right now
you would not recognize me.

It's not a trick. If you really look
there's nothing in my un-pixelated hands.

Catechism

Are the house sparrows twittering now? Yes.
Am I doing the dishes in preparation for a feast? Yes.
Am I already at the feast? Yes. Are the reluctant
participants, despite their reluctance, already
participating? Yes. Are the participants who rage
with resentment and defiance, who bloat with
righteousness and lust, also already participating?
Yes. Is Infinite Love upset, turned off, or
surprised by such tantrums? No. Does He or She
characterize them as sinful or wrong? No. He or She
waits until they're over, so you don't have to.
Am I already at the feast? Yes. As I mentioned,
there's no waiting involved. Can you win or lose
at the feast? Since everybody's already at the feast,
no. But if you'd like to, sure, go ahead, win or lose.
Is that the sound of my children waking up? Yes.
Are those my thoughts going on in my head? Yes,
they can always be. Do I actually think them
over and over? Yes. Is my misery as a result of
believing them part of the feast? Yes. A sideshow,
a minor diversion, perhaps, but definitely a part
of the overall celebration. Is an open, unheated can
of beans spooned out in an alleyway also a part
of the feast? Yes. Is circling the block for a parking
spot a part as well? Yes. How about going to work?
Yes. And riding the subway? Yes. And waking up
and going to sleep? Of course. What about deep
frustration and utter defeat? Definitely. Death? Yes.
Sitting on the couch and watching TV? Apparently.
Is trying to tell a difficult truth also part of the feast?
Yes, a big part. And lies, what about lies? Sure.

We Were Waiting For

1.

We were waiting for
Robin to show up.
The old furniture store
where Route 9 ends

in a shopping center
was now a mod
wine bar. The waiter
had a blotched and bloated face,

an occupational hazard,
I guess. We did not get
anything, but at Coney
Douglas and I went and saw

the opening of the ocean.
All the bathers line up
at the back of the beach
near the boardwalk and at

the sound of the gun run
to the water's edge
and dive in. 100s of
people but no Robin.

2.

It is an older house
and when you go
down to the basement
it opens up into

two Victorian sitting rooms
through which we walk.
French doors open out
onto a shady, lower terrace

in the woods where
we can just see
the back of what must be
my father's head.

The bald top of it
is sticking up from
the broad, floral-patterned
back of a stuffed

chair among some ferns,
and we are told
to approach with care
lest he turn and crumble.

3.

Traveling an ancient land
and in a building avoiding
pursuit down a metal
ladder I reach the bottom.

There's activity there,
a hag and an ogre.
I climb back up,
but he must've too,

for he peers in the doorway.
I hide in front of a closet
by putting my gray cloak
over me and sitting still.

This does not work.
They shout. He pulls out
his long serrated metal pole,
and I take out my

cane with a hook. His
arms are long and strong
and I try hooking his feet
and pulling. He grabs

the cane out of my hands
and beats himself with it,
laughing wildly to show me
he can't be hurt,

to make my courage and hope
by comparison paltry.

4.

At the beach in Jersey
I go deeper into the water.
There are vaguely menacing rocks
that I don't quite see,

and I don't want
to dive in and hit them.
The other people also go in,
happy at this time of year.

You can tell by their throwback faces
it's good for them
to flicker like a Super 8
movie telling me something

green and slimy and clustered,
something that clings to a rock and sways
like a pale head of hair
suspended in shallow water,

and somehow I'm off the hook.
This is the right beach.

5.

Two huge, pointed, Gothic archways
rising out of the ground,
the façade of a cathedral
the rest of which

has been lopped off,
or it's there, only its interior
has been infinitely expanded,
hidden, so that when

we enter through them
into this suddenly hilly,
sylvan paradise, we're surprised
and quieted. Our pace slows.

It's sunset, of course,
and as the winding
path we've chosen approaches
a crest we hear murmuring.

There is a gathering.
We walk down into the knoll
by the chapel and greet
the revelers. Candles are produced

and lit. We sit. After
the reading and the music,
we get up, and retracing our steps
along the wooded path

back out under the archways,
again we find ourselves
in the midst of hills
and trees. Again we find ourselves

under a terrific sky.
Again it is sunset.
There is a gathering
and candles being lit.

6.

The buildings are made of a dark
material and crowd the streets,
which are narrower, and the difference
between a map of the city

and the city, as we walked
in a drizzle from the Bronx
all the way down
to an old courthouse at the lower

edge of Manhattan, the harbor
waters sloshing against huge tarred
bulkheads, is slight. The bronze
doors are tall and heavy. We push

and go in. In the bleachers
is every kind of people, brought there
from the hothouses of Astroland,
where they were raised,

bottoming out on amusement,
especially for this purpose.
After a lengthy commotion,
we find out the usual Uncle,

known only to my Mom,
left a huge house in the Amboys
to my Mom, who was also
dead. There was nothing

left for us to do but leave
back out into the city.
An entire city
left to us but not enough.

7.

I am staying in a room
of maybe a hotel
in the middle of which
is a tent I sleep in.

When I come in
the next day the near side
of it is in tatters.
I try to fix the poles

which are made of bamboo
and are splintered. It sags,
and a trail of tatters
leads to another room

which is where the monster
sleeps. She is sleeping,
and two girls are standing
out in the carpeted hallway.

One of them comes up to me,
puts her arms around me,
and kisses me on the lips.
I actually levitate a little,

and when I alight say,
"That was nice."
There is an uncertain feeling
about what it meant

exactly and we walk
away from each other. Later,
when I come back
into the room the girl

is there. She knocks
three times and I realize
that that is the signal
for the monstrous proprietress

to wake and come.
Quickly I lay my broken
tent on the floor
and roll it up to go.

Plastic Bag

The wind blows open the door
and reaching in inundates the vessel

of your body. At first it's a thrill
to not have to bear burdens

or be of service, but to finally be
filled up with nothing at all,

and leaving gravity behind just fly
up and up, swoop and tumble,

shimmy and dance . . . But by then
you're thirty, forty stories up,

and looking through the tinted
glass you see a man at his desk.

His back is turned, and he's on
the phone in front of a computer,

when a sudden and opposite
gust catches you, swinging you

out over what is now an abyss,
and looking down you see

far below what is now a tiny
door beginning to shut.

You Can Always Pick It Back Up On The Way Out

It is a room,
and although you sometimes run there for protection
there are no bars on the windows,
nor is the door locked.
It is always open,
and although you can go there whenever you want,
pausing in the middle of whatever you are doing,
closing your eyes for a few moments,
there is never a line there waiting to go in.
The room is always empty
and ready for you to enter. Yet, before you do,
although you do not have to take off your shoes,
for the room loves your shoes and everything about you,
it is suggested you empty your pockets of fear,
which does not properly belong to you anyway,
and leave it in the threshold receptacle,
an article of furniture which is all the more prominent
in contrast to the wide and welcoming emptiness
you encounter as you enter,
for although you sometimes go there to catch your breath,
although you sometimes go there for comfort and rest,
although this room is always a refuge for your heart,
there are no chairs or couches or tables or rugs in the room.
There is no furniture there whatsoever.
The room is empty
and somewhat severe,
but in a simple and undemanding way that you encounter on your own,
for although you sometimes run to this room seeking communion,
although you sometimes go there to rejoin the human race,
and understand what you have in common with others,
especially your enemies,
nobody else is there,
and although therefore the prospect of entering this room
sometimes fills you with the dread of being alone,

especially with yourself, once inside the room,
(assuming, of course, you've left this trepidation at the door)
you do not feel lonely,
and although you may be perfectly contented there,
although you are never hungry or angry or ill-at-ease
while standing there looking out the window,
for on each of the four walls of the room is a window,
not the stained-glass or rose-colored or many-paned kind,
but the clearest and simplest,
the kind through which you can see a thing just as it is,
and see it as good,
and although you never grow tired of standing there looking out,
and although there are no rules for how long
you may stand there looking out,
you never stand there forever.
No, eventually you see something through the window,
something near or something in the distance,
and realize that that something is a thing
you might attend to, and you go.

Twenty-two Anticipatory Compensations

It's going to kill me,
this constant thinking about
what I did wrong,
what I could've done

differently, how my ambivalence,
instead of helping me
negotiate and navigate,
instead of helping me

avoid and avert, nearly cost me
my life. Under the circumstances,
it's easy to forget
all those beautiful verses,

all those yawning mornings
spent hammering out a line
or two. I am remembering especially
that one about becoming

a very old man
sitting in a room, the afternoon
sun coming through
a window, the walls papered

with all those beautiful verses
I'd been given to write.

Celtic Knot

Neither thrown out
nor buried in the backyard,
year-old lily bulbs,
a gift, indecisively secreted,

half-forgotten in the back
corner of the lower
refrigerator shelf, have begun,
blanched and blind,

to emerge (it's time!),
to push, coming up
against and then doubling back
against the perforated green

plastic bag they came in,
and remain in,
weaving in their cool
restricted dark

the repeated figure
of a question mark.

Offering

Take it out
of your head,

and put it in
the empty

wickedly grinning
half caved-in

month-old pumpkin head,
and carry the whole

decomposing mess,
the soft cavernous rot,

out into the back
yard and set it down

among the pale winter
stalks and sticks

and leave it there.
The bushy-tailed gray

gods will come
and eat it.

Awake and Sing

Largesse of Otter Fur

The pointlessness of pursuit
is just another illusion
to break up and grind under
the high heel of hard work

as if there were a total amount
of suffering to be doled out,
and by being tough and taking more
there's less for others.

The anointed highness of Beirut
instant justice for oil's legions
two hiccups and a grunting blunder
whose thigh feels what her heart would

active thwarts atonal counts
love buffering bee-bee war bouts
albeit enough of this god-forsaken bore
thin air's jest for mothers.

Grey-eyed

The great steps that go
up the Staten Island Terminal.
Russ and the boys come
the other way. Everything

is dark and Art Nouveau.
A stony Athena hangs her head
and a dimly lit green globe
rests on her shoulders.

Ugly ate the stop and go,
hup two, manhandled terra firma
while rusting dull buoys duh
and speedboats spray their druthers. Sing

or bark how hard you vote.
Bony concertinas bang their eyelids
and one random act sits, preens and dis-
robes lest we overhear older.

Chinatown

The members of the organization
wear friendly and earnest smiles.
They invite me to participate in
their end of year celebration.

Apparently my designation for the role
of sacrificial victim was pre-determined,
and their ever-helpful determination
in this regard is so profound I am

actually conflicted as I climb through
the small basement bathroom window.

Dented fenders and old organs shunned.
Near Wembley handsome fear rests and is tiled.
Day incites bees and hissing-hearted fate
therefore fends off what your accelerating ear won.

A parent leaves. Midas' indignant forty foot
pole and a sackful of dumb buzzes under.
Hope lever'd, meter shunned, industry
guards its isotopes and round iambs as

ashes leave flecks of desire, true or untrue,
tall bimbos and their wombs of wrath.

Crickets

The fir tree in front of me
rises directly out of what was
described on the web as a trout-stocked
lake, but now, in the flesh, appears

to be a half acre of standing water
and weedy muck, wildflowers and ferns,
crayfish and worms, bees, dragonflies
and frogs, the last of which is what

a girl with a long pole and net
repeatedly yelps as she scampers by
my picnic table, while her pink
faced and apologetic father plods

after her, the stub of a cigar
in his hand. All of which distinctions
the fir canopy's continuous waves
of chanting do and do not recognize.

Thirty-three love infants meet.
Ice eased. Reckless Ottawa fuzz,
dusky ribbony ebb, passed out and rocked,
bucked and buttoned, freshly in arrears.

Two peanut butter crackers understand
whatsoever you yuck. Mild-powered lanterns,
gray-ish and warm, be bragging rights
un-frocked, be that you do unto.

Eight pearls hide holes in an anklet.
A petit pois helps. Ashy canopy,
myopic apple of her eye, ink
erased, as apoplectic bother nods.

Half terror, half hubbub of my brother's
innocent head. Bald bewitching stink
defer unto me. Contains you. Us rave,
enchanting choo-choo de-narcotized.

Oops

I thought I was actually
interested in this other thing,
the world, its color and odor,
its taste, but really it was just

me putting the finishing touches
on a picture of me and my
sensations of this provisional
construct of words, my words.

Lies brought high Muzak
under house arrest, robin's nest mother's ring
which word fits over and under,
fits waste, utterly writ waste.

Keep uttering diminishing Anne Hutchison
aperture overly handed. Why
send a nation off its divisional
instructive herd? Why herd?

Over There

Jim at school, but 25 years later.
He talks to me like a manikin.
He is pleasant. His intentions are buried,
slightly receding. The possibility

that the power and the glory is something
I may participate in but do not,
and am not meant to, own, releases
me. Each breath buys you

a ticket. You may sit down now.
The show is about to begin.

Dim coolant be alive. Ears gather.
Trees walk with trees. Like Lee Marvin,
the Leica-manned ikon isn't whizzing
good or bad, but arbor'd, mightily beseeched.

The bossa nova military spat flowers,
end of story. For thine is the ape-hearted
fizzy-stated butternut and nutmeg—oops!—
only pleases. See tea death: defies to a now

and forever sticky wickets. Two nascent
wows and her boat comes about, again.

Safer

was a collection of people you knew,
and they were bigger because they were fewer,
and the colors were bright, more saturated and solid,
and beyond that were more people you could meet

one at a time and just as finite, and beyond that
there were dragons whose ability to fly and breathe fire
and terrorize the collection of people you knew
was directly proportional to the faith you placed in them,

and that faith was bright, more saturated and solid,
and so the dragons soared and were terrifically frightful
and also for a while haughtily impervious to the chips
called "selves" the borderless, highly partisan

organization calling itself "the pursuit of freedom"
began to plant in the chest, just to the left
of the heart, of every inhabitant it tracked down,
who, in turn, every time he or she looked

up at the empty sky and blinked, began to leech
and lose definition, began to multiply
at an astounding rate. Yes, the world was
a blue and green ball, steady and spinning.

Wafer

Huzzah! Confection's love be opal boo-boo.
Stand way, weird burgher of see-saw layered sewers.
Stand up, dolorous war might, war saturnine and stolid.
Stand around, weird fat warbling wood teeth.

Stop on a dime. Stand justly asinine. Stand around fat
terror wagons who ooze utility, who by-stand wreathes of ire.
Stand error eyes of chuckle. Bet on love be opal boo-boo.
Must wreck repro's optional doo-dah, wraiths' complacent thrum.

Stand about face; the Aye's write war saturnine and stolid.
Stand soda flagons stored. Stand war tariff's fiscal idols.
Stand alto forte oily ought, oily chimp. Stand nervy us,
chewed-up lips. Bald selves. The motherless sky leopard is

an origin whose eyes shine. All ringing bells, all pure roots,
every doomed vegan implant rusts, rests doo-dah's heft,
loves dumb art's never re-habb'd hidden split black gown.
Two interns' reverie on a dime hershey interlock.

Humpty-dumpty, I stand inked, bit into peach.
Stand oozed, ignited, bit into this stultified split
atom's accountant hate. I guess word huzzahs
anew stand: weened, tall, ready hand hitting.

Words won't
do anything

no matter
which ones

I choose
no matter

what order
I put

them in.
I have to

curl over
into my

dream and
sleep on

my side.

Weird birds
honk through

rainy spring.
Mad hatter

widgeons
the rich use

row water.
Disordered

caput
lemmings from

on high
heave to

the world's
boulder.

The wind's
two high

streams ran
deep as

money lied.

The Duh

The mouth of the bay
does not speak. The water
extends as far as it can
and covering the tongue of the bay

laps at the shells and sand,
and rocks of the shore.
For the shore is simply the place
where water ceases to be.

That word is over.
Forget about it. It
must've been
enough.

Amount loves away. A dozen
Topeka orders hex'd ends,
jazz forest's tin cans, handsome
lovers that stung love, today.

Tanned, lapsed Dashiell's sandman,
handsome mocks love's thrush,
or forth, sure his ample space
fears order, pieces rubies.

Fat world, his lover,
orbit and shout, "Hit! Hit!"
festive, keen
and tough.

Transparent

A man, collapsed in a beach chair,
sleeps. A silver cross,
hanging from his neck, hides
an area, precisely shaped
like itself, of skin on his chest,
that will not be pink
tomorrow. His two toddlers,
closer to the water, play
in the sand, while his slender
wife, in a matching chair
a few feet from him, watches.

From the outside ankle
of each chair a chain runs
and attaches itself to the inside
ankle of each of two other,
older and barely visible
children who, dressed up
in their years ago Sunday
best (it must be hot, if a little
transparent) stand and wait.

Trance Parents

Amen! Calling all past dinner peach dares!
All weepy hassled Wilbur Crosses!
All sanguine rum swizzles! All deckhands!
All hysteria priestly jelly rape!
Fuck it! Your next of kin honor fest
won't rot, won't keep ink.

Two narrow history tattlers
closet odor whose wonder by-ways,
India and Isles, were hassle-enders.
Life won. An un-hatching pair
of nephews freely thumping peaches.

Drums without wide thankless love
which peaches dare. A-train guns,
hands it matches. Fidel's toothy hindsight's
thankless love cheats love would rather

Bolder hands-on warily indivisible
chilling trend to fess up.
Thin ears fear. Oswego Sensei

tests litmus Bebop's iffy spittle:
tranced, spent, standard waif.

Homework

#3

Their wrists were cocked. The boat was coming about
the very buoy I was thinking of. My mind is frozen.
When you skate over it a little of it
on the surface melts and you glide, frictionless,
supported by the rest of it which goes down two feet
and is frozen. Who can hear it? You can hear it
toll in the distance. A sunny spot at the end
of a shady lane means hope, means not having to say
I want, means that takes the cake. She took the train
to get here but went back on a boat. "A guy like that,
you can just put him in and PLUNK he gets a hit,"
and that little bit of the surface melts and you skate
home, which means give me my reason,
which means that train of thought came to a grinding halt,
which means buoy, the lonely tolling of a rocking buoy,
a single seagull on top. I'm coming about.

#5

Once you've received the benefit of being forced
to wait your turn is it really necessary to speak?
Why do you eat? Why do you walk? An absurdly enthusiastic
love of enthusiasm on a bicycle peddling down a lane,
trees on either side. Such outer gear! Such
sunlight and shadow! It's nice to shake hands
with a stranger. It's nice to make a rubberband
stretch around danger. An idea. A single letter
separates friend from fiend. The two of them
sitting in a barn hoping to learn to love each other just a little
when the enormous owl's eyes opened and the walls
proved feathers. They began to ripple. I took a trip
down the stairs. The day awaited me
and my injury. Old rags tied to the tail of a kite
by a stranger, someone sitting under a tree, picnicking
of all things, paying no attention to these aerial feats.
Can you really just sit up and sing
the way birds begin to when the pie's been opened?

#6

Most of the houses on our street
are up in the trees. There's a robin's nest.
There's a squirrel's. A mockingbird's. Below,
a man parks, locks up, walks away.
He does not look up. The people
do not know they're the people.
The girl with the green eyes,
the boy from whose mouth obscenities bubble,
they do not look up. Is it possible?
The whole block is a seat they must
stand behind and wait. Someday
someone will surely come to sit
down and see if she likes it. At first the seed
grows down and what you see is only
the leafy afterthought of an impulse
that is dark and so wants to come
and sit and be with us. There is no rest
for our feet. Our branches point at
clouds we cannot read and at night
squirrels climb over our bodies
to get at the delicious and jagged
jack-o-lantern teeth on every stoop.

The thinking about it is blue.
The planning it out is blue.
Too? I live in a constant two,
a dim suspicion of recurrence
un-owned and all the subsequent lack
of reality implied. The hidden joke
here is that they're selling the book
as by a group of Americans who are "troubled."

The anticipation of reward is blue
whose clue comes from the pen itself,
what it wants to write and when.
Here I am, on the subway, a boy
in a man's body. When he says jump
I pull out my book and discuss
available dates. The approach
is blue. Two puppies
and their tail-wagging acuity.

Let's play a game. You put on a human suit
and I'll pretend the cube root
of your favorite number
is mine also. It's not. As a uniform
the wide brim hat is all the more ridiculous.
The event itself is not.

#8

There, on a street sign in the sunlight in the morning,
amid the parked cars and swept sidewalks,
among the pumpkins and chrysanthemums and cut-out ghosts,
while a passenger jet distantly roars overhead
and a newspaper thumps on the step, there, while turning
the corner onto the block, in the very midst of a ball
bouncing off the curb, of a bag of groceries in either arm,
in between a nod to a neighbor and a glance at the sky,
the hopeful November air, the air of wet and rot,
the chill air, there, on a street pole, just before
you manage to dig your keys out of your pocket,
after this thought but before the next, the letters
S-E-Z-E have been neatly and vertically spray-painted,
have been inserted between your left foot going forward
and then the right, there, something new,
an announcement, as if this were the coming of something
new, something dark and not to be entirely glad about,
as if this sunlight of children's voices were afloat
and suddenly slid to the side, exposing
the inner mechanisms of a huge clock
over the glinting metal of which one surviving arthropod crawls.

This is the line of a little off. This is the little
exhalation of a leaf. Go ahead and wave a flag
of your own choosing. Such gladness is not a thing
to wear or volunteer, is not the set piece
of a scooter left on the sidewalk, the whole thing
scooter and concrete and stoop, removed packed and shipped
to a museum to be re-assembled and lit. No,
its necessity was implanted in the fifteenth tooth
of the third cog and its floating world is one
among many, was notched to fit something else,
which it looks for and slides forward for,
like a little line of gladness.

She is talking black and that black drinks in the others.
Others are talking junk of which this edifice is built.
I don't mean junk. I mean that boat
that puts you in a frame of mind. Floating, floating

there are two others sitting in the kitchen.
They are not talking in a railroad
apartment. They are looking at each other. The apartment,
the building, the block, the whole neighborhood,

every brick of it, rests on a secret train,
even as we speak. The bricks speak
the way a crab might hide under a rock—oh,
those are bricks, they don't say anything—

and its movement's so smooth and continual
you can only sense its presence when it crashes
to a stop. "You, the one that climbed up
into a tree (there are no trees in this edifice!)

I see you. It's your stop." But instead of words,
when the old man clinging to the branches
opens his mouth in protest, one frog and then
another and then a third one comes out.

#11

It was as if the wind were carrying an agreed upon signal
from tree to tree, for everywhere you looked
branches had come to life and leaves were falling.
They were falling on your head and shoulders, on your shoes.
They were (all misty eyed) they were . . .
Invested in belief, the buttons pop.
"The Beltway," as if you could gird this "Republic's"
ever-expanding girth. They set up a tent in Bryant Park.
Inside, people were reading books by flashlight
as a statement. Beep beep. Back the truck up
and load this bed with talk. Here, boy! Here!

What do I intend? I don't. Someone else
takes care of that. He's the handyman, she said.
Unhand that wrist and count to ten. They are falling
on your head and shoulders. Hand him over
to the authorities whose arms are reaching up
through the piles of leaves. Kick at them
like a kid. Or think about it. Less an option
than a sentence. Before the judge but after the event,
or really after the judgment but before the event. Does the event
ever come? Before he died he was fun. Afterwards, too.
My arm is asleep, as they say. They are falling

and their all-at-once-ness mixes
with the memory of every other all-at-once,
so that it's not just circular but linear too,
a helix, a dizzying repetition of lessons
I get to try to wrap my mind around and practice
before the big test I kick at like a kid.

#12

He gets kicked in the shins all day long
so that when a kid walks up to him
and actually kicks him in the shins
it's a relief. It really happened. There was no smile,
no measuring of speech, which no amount of doing
or thinking about doing can wash away,
leave you clean. How do you feel? I feel great!
Not despite but because of the mess
on the table, the phone, in another country,
because our bodies are made of righteousness
that will not wash away, which is why
the convincing is a constant,
a hole in the bottom of a pocket
that, for instance, asks, "What does does do?"

After each new arrangement . . . No, before each . . . No,
for each new arrangement to be even possible,
the parts have to be picked up, put away. Disappeared,
ignorance has a right to be heard and understood,
to be stood under and held,
the weeping child to be rocked and witnessed,
not despite but because of the mess,
because our bodies are made of mud
that will not wash away, which is why
the because comes in a dark hat and umbrella.
The rain falls. A connection is made. A situation
averted in an untaught image. The equation
between the man and the small desert thistle,
the thistle and the sleeping man,

arms wrapped around a dull pillow of doing
or thinking about it while his soul slides away.

#14

Turn the lamp off. That's a little better.
Mere daylight. Now I don't feel so much like
I need to be about to. Like even though they say
otherwise it really isn't. Decant it. Decant it again.

You're so focused on the by now un-miraculous
regeneration of a torn-off limb that you don't
notice how even on the coldest clearest nights
the stars never penetrate the surface of the water

but reflect back and that afterthought at the bottom
will never suspect the destiny it's missing
and your tongue insists on uttering as if words
really were magic and you really could put play

in a pen and it would still be play and Kenneth Patchen
were an angel who actually throws a baseball
off the page and the dead were a line, straight as an arrow
and unending, and not a dimensionless dot.

#15

Suggestion is a robot.
Each of us is armed with a pencil.
When we form a line to fill out their forms
we think we can hear our own forms,
our skeletons rattle. Anticipation is a robot.

On a ball on the tip of a buttery
a kiskadee aims its toy beak at the sky
and sings like a pencil. This is,
as the adverb has it, suddenly
penetrating, and one writes it down,

of course, until the car out front
engaging leaves a skeleton
of smoke where a mind was. I forgot
to vote! Hurry up! The will of one's
equal to a vase which is a kind of car.

Look at it long enough and you're
the robot. You're in it
and you go. Through smoky layers
flamingoes are circumnavigating
its lacquered belly, a kind of daisy chain

that dances out content so that
disuse is use, is also a lonely robot.
That is why they put you up on a shelf,
well above that yellow arrangement of smoke,
the faintest pencil rising from your throat.

#16

Sometimes the root-heaved sidewalk sings
and a car door slams sublimely shut
just as an icicle falls from an eave and someone,
anyone in a brown winter coat is caught
descending a stoop (she'll be descending that stoop
forever), and her sister, the month-old silver-black
snow bank that has suddenly receded (and somehow
brightened a little) has left a revelation
of flattened bags, wrappers, and shit, yes,
the dogshit that is everywhere pulverized
and halfway to dirt sings too, as does its brothers,
the sky, the empty trees, whose new-found
manic angularity eases their long leaflessness
as if death were at last okay with itself,
and their children who gurgle under the glistening,
thinning ice and merrily run along the curb,
so that even my soggy feet seem to huzzah
my way across this drawbridge to somewhere
beyond the laundromat, then the pharmacy, then the post office
before the babysitter comes back with the kids.

#17

When I fell into the air
your telephone was in slow motion
and the city said "I am machine!"
and the ocean swollen
with the very opposite of soft
and beautiful faces of the dead.

When the city fell into the ocean
where were you?
I was machine
spitting out air to no avail
while the innumerable dead
talked their phones into falling.

The opposite of motion is a workshop
of the soft where the beautiful
dead become a single marble.
It rolls off a table and under a chair
where it stops and stares out,
the deep eye of the ocean.

When I fell into the air
You fell asleep. The soft of the ocean
was a machine that hid the bones
of the sharp workshop's dead,
swollen with beauty,
swollen with telephones.

#18

To be graced by the coming of a word
you didn't know you wanted. Thus our boat
set sail out of the harbor under the power
of its own wind, or rather one we'd summoned,
or rather humbly beseeched. This select-an-effect
is quick dried, saved from having to fall
back into human suspension for
one more day froze my tears. They are now
dice in a cup. Thus, we do not bluff
when we say, "Bring on the cold!"

Always it's, I put a pile of your things
on the stairs to go up so that the staying up
late reprieve plays itself out and even
sitting becomes thought of and chosen and
therefore hateful. Look at my eyes.
They're puffy. The Grim Reaper image implies
we're food, begging the question who
are we feeding and are they so worthy
of worship? When the news announced
again the unthinkable I wondered who

would be blamed and whether our Leader
would declare open-ended war on the fault
that had had the effrontery to shift (think
of the terrific pressure underneath it!), whether
a committee spokesperson would insinuate
that while the core, mantle and crust bore
some responsibility in unleashing the ocean,
sources say it was the Goddess Herself,
deep in Her dominion, behind it all, and whether
the Joint Chiefs would take an oath before

cameras (think of them as eager!) to hunt Her
down. Now think of a glass of mere water,
a picture of it on the front page of a paper. Now
breathe in and breathe out and let every other
image fall off your window ledge. The ledger
is mere wind that blows. That being right
is the wrong goal is demonstrated by the daughter
who brought her husband and five year old child
along when she went to stay with her mother
right after her father had died until things

settled down. After a few days of attending
to her mother, the daughter one night inexplicably
dies in her sleep. A week later the husband leaves
the child with his in-laws and drives their rental
into the unthinkable. That things don't settle
down is demonstrated by the miniature conifer
made of dried flowers and spray-painted gold
that sits at the center of the holiday table,
is demonstrated by the half-finished jig-saw puzzle
at the other end, is demonstrated by the fact

that yesterday I had something to put down
but today it's gone. Its location pressed, blurs
out of focus. What's left over? The child. Whatever
at any given moment hasn't been claimed
yet. Folded clothes. A toy boat. Some
stuffed animals. A pair of unthinkable shoes.

#19

If thoughts are energy and energy is matter,
and therefore nothing's destroyed, then, without interruption,
the things of this world, on the restless eyelids
of narcolepts, are being projected. When Justin Timberlake
clutches his crotch choreographically,
when fighter jets in formation sail overhead,
that is when these thoughts are dried and saved,
canned and shelved by our subaltern, the president,
who, kicked in the head by what he wanted
one too many times, was shrunk in size and given the position.
When I hopped up on the table and opened my throat
to sing, a bottle of wrong and right was poured into it
instead and I was stopped, instantly dried, and re-wound
in a flag to be played back later. That is why
when you're falling asleep you can hear, if you're saved,
the sudden inhalation of jars being opened.

#20

What I thought I knew but didn't.
What they tell you is true is a between the line
lubrication required for use, is the sound
a penny gives when it's squeezed.

After the birth of use I find myself
only in a kind of movie when I'm at
the beach. Beach. Waves crash
and my friends all call my other friend

Crash. The friction that ensues,
the fiction that imbues stops on a dime
and the blur flying in front of this well-oiled it
crashes off-screen. Scream. If I squint

I can see the sun has a faint but discernible
smiley face on it. I think. Penny. Pennies
from heaven but when one of them from that far up
hits you walking blithely below on the head . . . Eureka!

The idea of wariness or pity on my colleagues' faces,
the idea which was true: a high-necked indigo silk blouse
and a long string of jet black beads
the idea of establishing across the board blame

before taking action as opposed to the gratuitous
friends a puppy makes when it tells on itself,
when an embryo burrows
into the back of night and develops there

until a tiny, sharp-toothed puppy awakes
and barking breaks through the skin,
leaving a divot the size of a dime
between the wide, star-strung shoulders

of his mother. He puts on her dresses
and he looks good, her good.

#21

The plastic abdomen of the GI Joe,
the new one with the President's face,

is terrifically ripped. The dog's ears
stood up and the pancakes flipped

on their own as the blurry
flight patterns of the lapsed approached.

A security system salesman knocked.
The closing bell boulder rolled

into position and, except for that wild
west wanted poster here and there

affixed, the walls that are rising,
shoulder to shoulder, are unbroken

and shining. Separately, they are walking
on pink eggshells. She has a sinkful

before her (how the camera loves
the anxiety that seems to breathe

through her face!) while he (and this is a nod
to the silver age of silence) is out

behind the shed. Over and over,
without a sound except for the low

whirr of a projector, his ax head
swings through a pivoting sky

and bites into wood. This is called
an intentional face, a neat stack

of murderous and murdered thoughts.
This is called a piece of paper

that was terrifically ripped,
that was balled up and thrown at a basket,

but bouncing off the rim, missed.

#22

Put a pronoun here and we can begin: our
under the radar line of dominoes snaked its way
across the Atlantic around the Mediterranean to a secret location
reduced by daisy-cutters to an expanse of rubble
simple enough to be understood by the quantity
of paperwork required, and there, at that bright,
shining moment, stood at attention for,
as was mentioned, about a moment, and then,
after the mushroom flash of the distant camera,
toppled. Clackety-clack. The backs of the fallen
are the gear teeth of an enormous win-win machine,
which, because of the soft underbelly of its budget,
has been dimensionally down-sized to pay for
vacation. Whose? Uh-oh! This poem has to be
ripped up and re-written. The black and white backs
of the risen become the perfectly laid bricks
of a dream by a lake in a magazine you're
flipping through, become the stepping-stones of
wave after subsequent wave of carpet-bagging
bully materialists dressed up as Christians,
become the shining white teeth of a face
you can't quite place, become the headstones
knocked over in the middle of the night by Hate,
by empty-headed teenagers from Massapequa.

#23

The basis for membership is birth.
The basis for birth is having been not.
Even when it's not enough, it's enough.
The first, hopeful, as some say, to a fault
was superceded by a second and the second
by a third and so on. That is how
they came to be details, people living
somewhat inland from the coast.
Isolated by being delivered, surrounded by
the memory of a sensation of a question
which unanswered hardens, this hopefulness,
this small town thing-ness (thing is dead!
long live ness!) becomes one among many
numbered chips to pick up and weigh.
What about this one? And that? Meanwhile
the mind coasts and the underlying lack,
dressed up as an apple and a nap,
grows jealous, picks up the phone. Hello?
Slowly the non-idea of being here
on an impermanent basis, and that is
the basis. You had no idea the whole time
(and that whole-ness is a film being projected
by you and for you but you were asleep,
coasting) you were already a member
of a club that meets each morning, each in his secret,
and isolated (this is part of the there's-
already-enough-of-you plan) location to lift
its voice. Heave ho! How quickly from trying
to figure out how to do a good job following to being led
regardless. The sweet soft focus of uselessness,
the wave's ruthless indifference to personality
was an occasion for cheer. Here we are, all dressed up
sitting around a ravaged table. We've outlasted
the kitchen and the waitstaff. The maître d'

tells us before turning out the lights we're welcome
to spend the night. The simplicity of a life,
how it might be spent and how it must be
taken away in all cases was an occasion
for glee, for having been not. To be focused
take your hand from the dial and do not domesticate
the dark. There is already a voice
that is, syllable by syllable, somewhat reliable,
but only on a need to know basis.

#24

The present could not have come any sooner.
You say yours is the fastest? Well, the shortest
distance between this apocalypse and the next
is the next step into thin air. It's getting

sunnier and more obvious. We vote for the biggest
and simultaneously the smallest, now, without saying
please. This is the happiest moment of my life.
No, this is the happiest. The moment was

black and rectangular. We jumped in.
It couldn't have been any kinder. It's getting
colder and more delicious. Soon, no one
will be able to cast a ballot or leave.

Deep into enemy territory the Sooners marched,
without saying please. This is the happiest
moment of my life. I drank a pint of paint thinner.
That's how I got here. No, this is.

#25

I dislike having to write these sentences.
Any project, conceived of as a kind of campaign
(political, military or otherwise), with its attendant
arm-twisting and compulsive positioning, makes one un-free
and to that exact un-monosyllabic degree, unhappy.

Instead, of the small band of cloaked travelers
just one stepped forward and offered, "I dislike the having
of having to write these sentences." The keeper
of the gatehouse then took this password and the narrow
slot in the timbered door slid shut. The group waited.

Instead, today, I could take a walk or get on the subway.
I could misplace myself or make myself unsafe
for enrichment, for birthday lists and little magazines,
for preschool subcommittee meetings on accountability,
for the heavy ancient golden worm that he wore

on his middle finger. The great flattened ball of the sun
touched the western hills. He, when he saw them,
turned out of the road and made toward that boggy bottom
where finally it was midnight. All the talking at me
voices erased, swallowed up. When I sit down

with this uncovered silence I feel the unjust joy
in having been taken on to re-write a blank page and wonder
how come when you disobey them they say
you're not listening, when in fact you've heard them
loud and clear. A shawl of blue pale gauze

sprinkled with little diamonds and edged with a fringe
of rose pink silk. The stringed instruments begin
now, preluding in parts.

#32

Even the desolations of November have been erased
by further desolation. Good clean death,
gold and violet death, our necessary consolation. Yes,
put a username here in place of the real one
that has no compunction but bleeds itself white.
The usual close-ups of thickened tongues,
of gray stubbly fields and bones picked clean,
melt, spreading a viscous puddle of unmeaning
that begins to drip down a staircase, which is circular,
which is over the top (lo! the footfalls descend!)
but continuous. You step over it. It turns and turns out

Jack and the Beanstalk was a story to climb up,
Augustus Gloop was a name to laugh at,
and therefore a life was a something to do something
to? With? Alongside? Kiss me
goodbye. Good boy. Now go outside
and get some disinterested sun. Pour it over
your blistering palms and pulpy eyes,
over a life that was
not more or less than a single soul
wagered on a single thought, a roll of the die. Lose
the explanatory violet and gold. Offer it over

the yawning dark. The talk. What
did you say? Gum, gum, and ordinary gum.

Why I Like to Garden

A hardy native American
Rocky Mountain Columbine
grows wild at high elevations
but is equally at home
in more temperate regions.
Its light violet petals
form a showy collar
around its brilliant white
interior cup. This tough
yet delicate plant doesn't pack
heat or hold a grudge,
and it's nice to think
the Colorado State Flower
was a common enough sight
for Neil or Jack.

Brightly colored and densely
packed flower clusters
on strong stems, Sweet
William is a perennial
in some climates. In areas
where it is biennial
replant in mid-summer
for flowers each spring.
Keep young plants
evenly moist, for they
are neither dry nor bitter,
neither self-servingly irresolute
nor mechanically ironic.
Of course, you may know
Sweet William by his other
names: Catchfly, Phlox
Maculata, or Heart's Ease.

Alaska Shasta Daisy is a
splendid plant for perennial
borders and early-summer
cut flowers. The bright white
blossoms and sunny yellow
centers bring a cooling
accent to hot June days.
Very hardy. Grows wild
in those areas unfrequented
by man. Doesn't give a
moment's thought to what
we think. Keep flowers
cut to extend season.

Lacy sprays of dainty blooms
covering mound-like dwarf
plants, Forget-me-nots neither
endorse nor oppose any causes.
Clusters of delicate sky-blue
blossoms blooming profusely
in moist, partly shaded locations,
Forget-me-nots are a gentle
and open-ended invitation
to remember the possibility
that we might not know.
Adds delicate beauty to beds
and borders. Very effective
when massed alongside Achillea,
Columbine, or Coreopsis.

Delightful mounding plants
with cheery blue flowers
from midsummer until frost,
the Dwarf Morning Glory
is ideal for sunny borders,
hanging baskets and patio planters.
While related to the common
vining Morning Glory, the Dwarf
does not colonize vast vertical
spaces, does not climb on,
entwine and choke its neighbor
in the so-called open and free
competition for life. No,
the sun shines equally on all,
and this plant is happy to bloom
in its appointed spot,
is delighted to blossom early
and decahedrally in its secure,
dry and sunny bed.

A hardy and low-growing
perennial with eye-popping
red flowers on top of
blue ever-green foliage, Pink
Maiden Dianthus Brilliant
is perfect for rock gardens
and borders, and boasts
a superfluity of names. This
abundance of dainty identities
are clustered and communal,
are disarmed and peripheral
and pink. Think of Christ,
how he tells his followers
to turn the other cheek,
or of Mary Magdalene,
how she shears her Lord's
Dianthus back to half-size
after flowering to encourage
the fullest blossoming.

Dainty sky-blue flowers
on gracefully arched stems
rising from clumps of
delicate-looking foliage,
Flax is attractive in masses
and useful for borders
as an accent in foundation
plantings. Plant in spring
or fall for bloom the following
summer. If you love blue,
if you haven't abandoned dusk
and darkness, nor wish
to live in unambiguous
and non-multiple denial,
if your pockets aren't full
of stubs and receipts,
then maybe this flower,
abutting areas of Little Johns,
Balldons, or Aster Alpine
Blues, will please you.

Thousands of dainty white
flowers create a cloud-like
effect on top of this bushy
perennial. Snow White
Baby's Breath makes
an attractive background
planting, and, unlike fossil fuel
combustion, Baby's Breath
is white and silent, turns
exhaustion into a joy
that is warm and moist,
and does this deep
restorative work while abed
and asleep. A great filler
for bouquets. Cut back
branches as soon as flowers
are fully open, and leave
every vapory idea
on the editing room floor.

Masses of flowers in sapphire,
blue, crimson, rose, lilac
and white, an impressive display
all season long, Lobelia
is easy to grow from seed,
is derived from some once referred to
but now impossible to locate
Shakespearean apocrypha. The runt
of the litter, a younger sister,
displaced by bald rivalry,
crazed by narrative's hunger
for winners and losers, for
obvious-as-a-thumb hydrangeas
and weeds, this multi-colored
orphan can have a home
in my 15 by 15 foot backyard
garden. Welcome, Lobelia!

Small, red trumpet-like flowers
open from dusk to early morning
on glossy, vertical waves of
multi-fingered green foliage.
This densely growing aggressive
climber all over the city
civilizes the chain link fences
between neighbors. The small flower
does not blow its own horn,
but is a clarion call to assemble,
each on his separate side,
and at the end of day wonder
at such red together, and thus to offer up
small talk where there otherwise
might be none. Please note:
Cardinal Cypress Climber Vine
seed has a hard seed coat.
To aid in seed germination
nick or cut seed coat
with a nail file and soak
seed overnight.

Eight to ten inch lemon-colored
fantasies top this tall sunflower
in mid-summer. Great for hedges
and tall borders. Easy to grow,
this monstrous effusion of yellow
petals and dense, velvety seeds
values, like Van Gogh, intensity
over subtlety of vision, knocking
us (because we need to be)
over the head with the reminder
that there is no euphemism
for God. Say it. If that isn't
enough, in late August, squirrels,
sometimes two at a time,
to demonstrate what being one
might be, leap from a fence
to an already top-heavy seed pod,
and the six foot plant topples
and crashes in Goliath-like ruin,
seeds scattering over beds,
scavengers scrambling to feast,
removing the "my" from garden.

Royal White Sweet Pea
produces an abundance
of sweetly perfumed flowers
on vigorously climbing vines.
Blooms in late spring,
perfect for covering fences
and trellises with empty,
glistening white color. Seed
depth 1". Seed space 2".
Thin space 6". Height 5-6'.
Sprouts in 10-20 days. Sweet Peas
blossom most freely when sown
in rich soil, when buried alive,
when kept out of sight,
when we pray for the humility
to acknowledge our utter
redundancy. Blindingly white,
they rise out of the ground
and ride by on horseback
while we hide behind a hedge.

Thomas Jefferson loved the beautiful
trusses of tall, old-fashioned
Cleome in his renowned flower
gardens in Monticello. Today,
these vigorous summer flowers
are treasured in restoration
and heirloom gardens. Today, outright
bondage is no longer the delicate
bloom of our economic system.
Today, you try to wake up
from the past but instead hum
Onward Christian Soldiers
while all around you the invisible
infrastructure of trust crumbles,
while ravenous hummingbirds pierce
Color Fountain Cleome's unique
blossoms with their long
pink petals and spidery stamens
that clutch at air. Space
seedlings 12 to 14 inches
apart to give the dominant
plants room to mature.

Now the famous flavor
and heavy pole yield come
in bush form. Large plump
green pods reaching six
to seven inches long.
Great for canning, freezing
or fresh use, the Kentucky
Wonder is also great
for its time elapsed
stop action and lack
of certainty, for its miniscule
moments and largesse of wonder;
for it has turned over
not just its small tendrils
and spade-shaped leaves,
not just its stout roots
and fruited clusters,
but the whole enterprise,
its burgeoning, ascending all,
so that its life is now
none of its business, but is
or does, if that distinction
could still be said to apply.

Traditionally used in a tea
or tincture as a tonic
to calm nerves, alleviate stress
due to anxiety. So let go
of the kind of automatic thinking
that separates words like "wort"
and "mother." They go together
easily and beautifully if only
you'd follow these simple tips:
direct seed in mid-spring;
keep seed bed evenly moist
during germination, well-watered
through maturity; pre-emptively
give up the glory and thus
the whole idea of credit
(you may have to forego
your craving for win-win
situations) by harvesting before
the flower-heads form
(and your native curiosity)
and their delicate purple pink
(you'll have to take my word
on this on faith) flowers
blossom for serenity to steep
into the steaming cup.
Now repeat, but simply,
without the parentheses.

Exceptionally sweet, deep red flesh
hides behind a distinctively
dark green striped rind. Round
and tough as a centurion's
sandal they grow in a mere
matter of weeks up to 25
pounds! Now, that's a big
slippery, crimson sweet baby
Demeter suffers you to take
(She has so many) in your arms
and severing its cord run off with
to your kitchen and kitchen knives
where you chop it up on a counter
and put the pieces on a platter
to feed the many yelping mouths
that have run around all afternoon
playing games half-formed
by market forces and media
campaigns in the hot Tuscan sun.
It is the month of Julius
Caesar, suffer yourself the pleasure
to sow six seeds over a hill
9 to 10 inches across. When plants
are well-established, you are ready
to thin, transplant and begin
your new colonies. This packet will
sow approximately seven hills.